Decoding the TOEFL® iBT

Advanced

SPEAKING

INTRODUCTION

For many learners of English, the TOEFL® iBT will be the most important standardized test they ever take. Unfortunately for a large number of these individuals, the material covered on the TOEFL® iBT remains a mystery to them, so they are unable to do well on the test. We hope that by using the *Decoding the TOEFL® iBT* series, individuals who take the TOEFL® iBT will be able to excel on the test and, in the process of using the book, may unravel the mysteries of the test and therefore make the material covered on the TOEFL® iBT more familiar to themselves.

The TOEFL® iBT covers the four main skills that a person must learn when studying any foreign language: reading, listening, speaking, and writing. The *Decoding the TOEFL® iBT* series contains books that cover all four of these skills. The *Decoding the TOEFL® iBT* series contains books with three separate levels for all four of the topics as well as the *Decoding the TOEFL® iBT Actual Test* books. These books are all designed to enable learners to utilize them to become better prepared to take the TOEFL® iBT. This book, *Decoding the TOEFL® iBT Speaking Advanced*, covers the speaking aspect of the test. It is designed to help learners prepare for the Speaking section of the TOEFL® iBT.

Decoding the TOEFL® iBT Speaking Advanced can be used by learners who are taking classes and also by individuals who are studying by themselves. It contains three parts and forty units. Part A covers the Independent Speaking Task (Question 1) while Part B and Part C cover the Integrated Speaking Tasks (Questions 2-4). There is also one actual test at the end of the book. Each unit has either two independent questions or two integrated questions. It also contains exercises designed to help learners understand how to present the best possible responses for the Speaking section. The passages and questions in *Decoding the TOEFL® iBT Speaking Advanced* are the same difficulty levels as those found on the TOEFL® iBT. Individuals who use *Decoding the TOEFL® iBT Speaking Advanced* will therefore be able to prepare themselves not only to take the TOEFL® iBT but also to perform well on the test.

We hope that everyone who uses *Decoding the TOEFL® iBT Speaking Advanced* will be able to become more familiar with the TOEFL® iBT and will additionally improve his or her score on the test. As the title of the book implies, we hope that learners can use it to crack the code on the TOEFL® iBT, to make the test itself less mysterious and confusing, and to get the highest grade possible. Finally, we hope that both learners and instructors can use this book to its full potential. We wish all of you the best of luck as you study English and prepare for the TOEFL® iBT, and we hope that *Decoding the TOEFL® iBT Speaking Advanced* can provide you with assistance during the course of your studies.

Michael A. Putlack
Stephen Poirier
Tony Covello

TABLE
OF
CONTENTS

ABOUT THE TOEFL® iBT SPEAKING SECTION

How the Section Is Organized

The Speaking section is the third part of the TOEFL® iBT and consists of four questions. Question 1 is called the Independent Speaking Task and asks test takers to speak about a familiar topic. The other questions, questions 2-4, are called the Integrated Speaking Tasks. These tasks require test takers to integrate their speaking skills with other language skills such as listening and reading skills.

For each of the four questions, test takers are given preparation time and response time. During the preparation time, test takers can write down brief notes about how they will organize their responses. The preparation time ranges from 15 to 30 seconds, and the response time is either 45 or 60 seconds. The spoken responses are recorded and sent to be scored by raters. The raters evaluate responses based on three criteria: Delivery (how clear your speech is), Language Use (how effectively you use grammar and vocabulary to convey your ideas), and Topic Development (how fully you answer the question and how coherently you present your ideas).

Changes in the Speaking Section

The Speaking section is the section that has gone through the most drastic changes. Two question types – Questions 1 and 5 on the old test – have been removed. Therefore, the total number of questions has become four instead of six. Accordingly, the time allotted for the Speaking section has been reduced from 20 minutes to 17 minutes. However, the remaining questions have no changes, and the preparation times and the response times remain the same.

Question Types

TYPE 1 Independent Speaking Task: Question 1

The first question asks test takers to speak about a familiar topic. It is necessary for test takers to include specific examples and details in their response. After the question is presented, test takers are given 15 seconds to prepare their response and 45 seconds to speak.

Question 1 asks test takers to make a personal choice between two possible opinions, actions, or situations. In addition, on recent tests, test takers are sometimes given three options from which to choose, and they may be asked to speak about both the advantages and the disadvantages of a particular topic. Test takers are required to explain their choice by providing reasons and details. Topics for this question include everyday issues of general interest to test takers. For example, the question may ask about a preference between studying at home and studying at the library, a preference between living in a dormitory and living in an off-campus apartment, or a preference between a class with a lot of discussion and one without discussion.

ABOUT THE TOEFL® iBT SPEAKING SECTION

TYPE 2 Integrated Speaking Tasks (Reading, Listening, and Speaking): **Questions 2 and 3**

The second and third questions require test takers to integrate different language skills. Test takers are first presented with a short reading passage. The time given for reading is 45-50 seconds. After that, test takers will listen to a conversation or a lecture which is related to information presented in the reading passage. They need to organize their response by using information from both the reading passage and the conversation or lecture. For these questions, test takers are given 30 seconds to prepare their response and 60 seconds to speak.

Question 2 concerns a topic of campus-related interest, but it does not require prior firsthand experience of college or university life in North America to understand the topic. The reading passage is usually between 75 and 100 words long. It may be an announcement, letter, or article regarding a policy, rule, or future plan of a college or university. It can also be related to campus facilities or the quality of life on campus. After reading the passage, test takers will listen to two speakers discuss the topic presented in the reading passage. Typically, one of the two speakers shows a strong opinion about the topic. On recent tests, however, speakers have shown mixed feelings about the topic, so they like it yet also dislike some aspect of it. Test takers need to summarize the speaker's opinion and the reasons for holding it.

In Question 3, test takers will read a short passage about an academic subject and then listen to a professor lecture about that subject. The question requires test takers to relate the reading passage and the lecture. Topics for this question can be drawn from a variety of fields, including life science, social science, physical science, and the humanities. However, the question does not require prior knowledge of any particular field.

TYPE 3 Integrated Speaking Task (Listening and Speaking): **Question 4**

The last question presents only a listening passage—a lecture—and not a reading passage. Test takers need to respond based on what they hear. They are given 20 seconds to prepare their response and 60 seconds to speak.

For Question 4, test takers will listen to a lecture about an academic topic. As in Question 3, topics for this question can be drawn from a variety of fields, including life science, social science, physical science, and the humanities. Again, no prior knowledge is necessary to understand the lecture. After hearing the lecture, test takers are asked to summarize the lecture and to explain how the examples are connected with the overall topic.

HOW TO USE THIS BOOK

Decoding the TOEFL® iBT Speaking Advanced is designed to be used either as a textbook in a classroom environment or as a study guide for individual learners. There are 3 parts and 40 units in this book. Each unit provides 2 sample questions, which enable you to build up your skills on a particular speaking task. At the end of the book, there is one actual test of the Speaking section of the TOEFL® iBT.

Part A — Independent Speaking Task

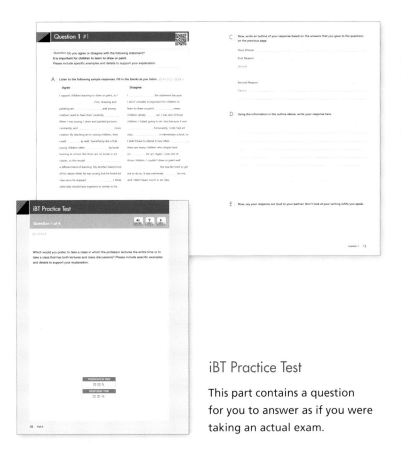

This section has a Speaking question followed by sample responses with blanks for you to fill in as you listen to them. This is followed by brainstorming questions and spaces to write an outline and a sample answer.

iBT Practice Test

This part contains a question for you to answer as if you were taking an actual exam.

Part B — Integrated Speaking Tasks: Reading, Listening, and Speaking

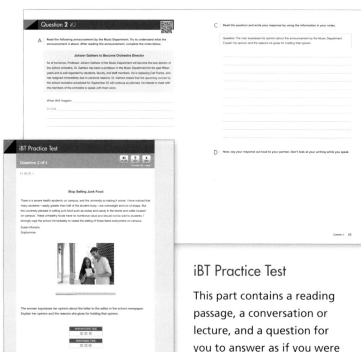

This part has a reading passage followed by either a conversation or lecture. There are spaces to take notes on the passage and the conversation or lecture. This is followed by a space to write your own sample answer.

iBT Practice Test

This part contains a reading passage, a conversation or lecture, and a question for you to answer as if you were taking an actual exam.

Part C — Integrated Speaking Task: Listening and Speaking

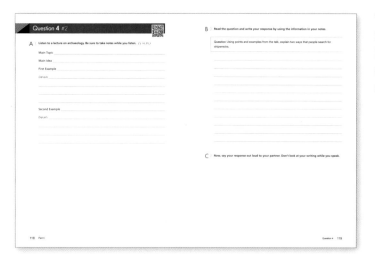

This part has a lecture. There is space to take notes on the lecture. This is followed by a space to write your own sample answer.

iBT Practice Test

This part contains a lecture and a question for you to answer as if you were taking an actual exam.

● **Actual Test** (at the end of the book)

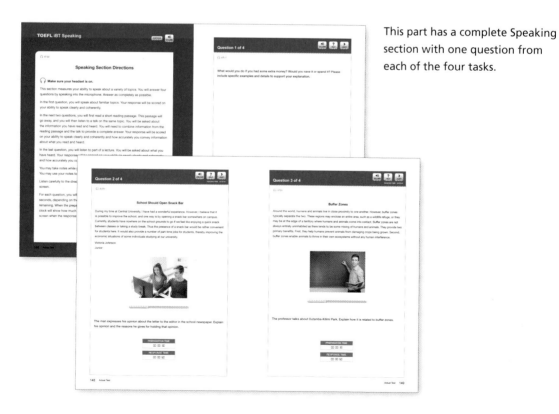

This part has a complete Speaking section with one question from each of the four tasks.

Independent Speaking Task
Question 1

Independent Speaking Task

◢ About the Task

The Independent Speaking Task asks you to speak about familiar topics. It is necessary for you to include specific examples and details in your responses. After each question is presented, you are given 15 seconds to prepare your response and 45 seconds to speak.

The Independent Speaking Task is the first question (question 1) of the Speaking section.

Question 1 asks you to choose between two possible opinions, actions, or situations and then to explain why you made that choice by providing reasons and details. Common topics are everyday issues that are of general interest. Many questions provide a statement and ask if you agree or disagree with it while others simply ask you which option you prefer. These questions may ask about a preference between studying art and playing sports or a preference between joining a club and working part time.

When you answer the question, be sure to use examples. Personal examples involving family members are ideal. The examples you use do not have to be actual events that occurred, but you should present them that way. You merely need to provide examples that defend the argument you are making. In addition, do not discuss both sides for the question. Make your choice and speak only about it.

◾ Sample Question

🎧 Q1_00_1

Do you agree or disagree with the following statement?

It is healthier to cook food at home than to eat out at restaurants.

Please include specific examples and details to support your explanation.

PREPARATION TIME
00:00:15

RESPONSE TIME
00:00:45

Sample Response   🎧 Q1_00_2

I fully agree with the statement for two reasons. First, when you eat at home, you can control every ingredient in the food you consume, but you can't do that at restaurants. My family almost always eats at home, and my mom is careful about only using healthy ingredients. As a result, everyone in my family is in good physical condition and has no health problems. Second, when you eat at home, you often eat less than you do at restaurants. At home, when I'm full, I stop eating because I know we can save the leftovers and eat them later. Since everyone in my family does this, none of us is overweight, so we're all healthy.

Question Do you agree or disagree with the following statement?

It is important for children to learn to draw or paint.

Please include specific examples and details to support your explanation.

A | Listen to the following sample responses. Fill in the blanks as you listen. 🎧 Q1_01_1 / Q1_01_2

Agree

I support children learning to draw or paint, so I _____ . First, drawing and painting are _____ , and young children need to have their creativity _____ . When I was young, I drew and painted pictures constantly, and _____ more creative. By teaching art to young children, they could _____ as well. Something else is that young children often _____ by book learning at school. But there are no books in art classes, so this would _____ a different kind of learning. My brother hated most of his classes when he was young, but he loved art class since he enjoyed _____ . I think other kids would have experiences similar to his.

Disagree

I _____ the statement because I don't consider it important for children to learn to draw or paint. _____ , many children simply _____ art. I was one of those children. I hated going to art class because it was _____ . Fortunately, I only had art class _____ in elementary school, so I didn't have to attend it very often. _____ , there are many children who simply have no _____ for art. Again, I was one of those children. I couldn't draw or paint well _____ the teacher tried to get me to do so. It was extremely _____ for me, and I didn't learn much in art class.

B | Think about the following questions. Use your answers to them to help you organize your thoughts.

Agree

1 Why should children learn to draw or paint?
2 How can they benefit from drawing or painting?
3 How is art class different from other classes at school?

Disagree

1 Why shouldn't children have to learn to draw or paint?
2 How do many children like art class?
3 How do children who can't do art well feel?

C   Now, write an outline of your response based on the answers that you gave to the questions on the previous page.

Your Choice

First Reason

Details

Second Reason

Details

D   Using the information in the outline above, write your response here.

E   Now, say your response out loud to your partner. Don't look at your writing while you speak.

iBT Practice Test

🎧 Q1_01_3

Which would you prefer, to take a class in which the professor lectures the entire time or to take a class that has both lectures and class discussions? Please include specific examples and details to support your explanation.

PREPARATION TIME
00:00:15

RESPONSE TIME
00:00:45

> **Question** Do you agree or disagree with the following statement?
> **Everyone eighteen years of age or older should be allowed to vote.**
> Please include specific examples and details to support your explanation.

A | Listen to the following sample responses. Fill in the blanks as you listen. 🎧 Q1_02_1 / Q1_02_2

Agree

I _____ the statement that everyone eighteen years of age or older should be allowed to vote. _____, people who are eighteen are _____ in most countries around the world. They should therefore be _____ in all manners. One way to treat them properly is to _____. Something else to consider is that people who are eighteen years of age _____ join the military in my country. My country's government obviously trusts eighteen-year-olds to _____. If a person is old enough to fight for his or her country, then that person should also _____ _____ old enough to participate in elections by voting.

Disagree

I _____ that people who are eighteen years of age or younger should be allowed to vote. Instead, I think the voting age should be either twenty or twenty-one. _____ a person who is eighteen might be physically mature but is not yet _____ or _____ _____ mature. Elections are important, but young people are often persuaded to vote for the candidates who make the most promises to them. Of course, these politicians don't intend to _____, but teenagers don't know that, so they get tricked. _____ most eighteen-year-olds still live with their parents. If they are not independent and able to support themselves, then they _____ voting in any elections.

B | Think about the following questions. Use your answers to them to help you organize your thoughts.

Agree

❶ Why should people eighteen or older be allowed to vote?

❷ What rights do people eighteen or older have?

❸ What rights should people eighteen or older have?

Disagree

❶ Why shouldn't people eighteen or older be allowed to vote?

❷ How do many people in their late teens act?

❸ What is the ideal voting age?

C Now, write an outline of your response based on the answers that you gave to the questions on the previous page.

Your Choice _____

First Reason _____

Details _____

_____

Second Reason _____

Details _____

_____

D Using the information in the outline above, write your response here.

_____

_____

_____

_____

_____

_____

_____

_____

E Now, say your response out loud to your partner. Don't look at your writing while you speak.

🎧 Q1_02_3

Some teachers want their students to sit in the same seats every day. Others like to have their students change seats regularly. Which do you think is better and why? Please include specific examples and details to support your explanation.

PREPARATION TIME
00:00:15

RESPONSE TIME
00:00:45

Question Do you agree or disagree with the following statement?

Newspapers are better resources than television when it comes to delivering news about current events.

Please include specific examples and details to support your explanation.

A | **Listen to the following sample responses. Fill in the blanks as you listen.** 🎧 Q1_03_1 / Q1_03_2

Agree

I agree with the statement _____ _____. The first is that newspapers can provide more _____ of current events than television can. When a newsworthy event occurs, newspapers can run _____ about it, but a television program might only _____ about it for a couple of minutes. _____, now that most newspapers have websites, they can provide virtually _____ of information about a single event. _____, there was an election in my country recently, and the papers provided long, detailed articles about it. Most people were _____ the news they got from the papers, but they complained about the _____ in news reports on television.

Disagree

I disagree with the statement and _____ _____ television is better than newspapers at delivering news on current events. _____ is that television can show video and audio images of events _____ newspapers can't. There were some big protests in my country last month. The TV stations _____, so viewers saw the events as they occurred. The newspapers couldn't do that. _____ is that TV news programs often hire experts to provide commentary on events as they happen. These individuals can explain the _____ of events and how they might have positive or negative _____. This provides viewers with _____ from experts.

B | **Think about the following questions. Use your answers to them to help you organize your thoughts.**

Agree

1. What makes newspapers better than television?
2. What kinds of reports can newspapers run?
3. What's an example of when a newspaper reported on current events better than television did?

Disagree

1. What makes television better than newspapers?
2. What kinds of reports can television show?
3. What's an example of when a television station reported on current events better than a newspaper did?

C Now, write an outline of your response based on the answers that you gave to the questions on the previous page.

Your Choice _____

First Reason _____

Details _____

_____

Second Reason _____

Details _____

_____

D Using the information in the outline above, write your response here.

_____

_____

_____

_____

_____

_____

_____

_____

E Now, say your response out loud to your partner. Don't look at your writing while you speak.

iBT Practice Test

🎧 Q1_03_3

Do you prefer to communicate with others face to face or by email? Please include specific examples and details to support your explanation.

PREPARATION TIME
00:00:15

RESPONSE TIME
00:00:45

> **Question** Do you agree or disagree with the following statement?
> **Universities should encourage their students to join clubs.**
> Please include specific examples and details to support your explanation.

A | Listen to the following sample responses. Fill in the blanks as you listen. 🎧 Q1_04_1 / Q1_04_2

Agree

I agree with the statement for two reasons. Firstly, students shouldn't _____ their studies while at a university. Instead, they ought to become well-rounded individuals _____ their studies and other activities. They can do this _____ or two. My older sister joined clubs at her university and felt that her club activities _____ as a person. Secondly, universities should _____ students to join clubs because membership will improve the _____ of many students by letting them make new friends. Too many students attend universities and only make one or two friends. _____, they feel lonely and don't enjoy themselves. They can _____ by joining clubs though.

Disagree

I _____ the statement because I don't want universities to _____ students to join clubs. _____, students should attend universities to learn, so they ought to focus on their studies. _____ joining clubs, students should take _____ they can. My brother didn't join any clubs but _____ of classes every semester. He got a great education and doesn't _____ his decision at all. Something else _____ is that many students join clubs and then _____ their studies in favor of their social lives. This _____ my brother's roommate. He joined three clubs and made lots of friends. _____, he spent too much time meeting them, so his grades _____ .

B | Think about the following questions. Use your answers to them to help you organize your thoughts.

Agree

1. What can students learn from joining clubs?
2. How else can students benefit from being members of clubs?
3. What are some examples of how students benefited from their club memberships?

Disagree

1. Why should students avoid joining clubs?
2. How can clubs interfere with students' educations?
3. What can happen if students belong to too many clubs?

C | Now, write an outline of your response based on the answers that you gave to the questions on the previous page.

Your Choice _____

First Reason _____

Details _____

_____

Second Reason _____

Details _____

_____

D | Using the information in the outline above, write your response here.

_____

_____

_____

_____

_____

_____

_____

_____

_____

E | Now, say your response out loud to your partner. Don't look at your writing while you speak.

iBT Practice Test

Q1_04_3

Which do you prefer, to have classes in the morning or in the afternoon? Please include specific examples and details to support your explanation.

PREPARATION TIME
00:00:15

RESPONSE TIME
00:00:45

Question 1 #5

Question Some students prefer to review the material they learn in their classes regularly. Others prepare to review the material all at one time. Which do you think is better and why? Please include specific examples and details to support your explanation.

A | Listen to the following sample responses. Fill in the blanks as you listen. 🎧 Q1_05_1 / Q1_05_2

Review the Material Regularly

Most of my friends prefer to review the material _____, but I don't. I like reviewing the material regularly. I _____ I feel I can remember the material better by going over it the same day I learn it at school. _____ the information is still fresh in my mind, I can _____ my memory and then _____ recall it in the future. I also like reviewing the material frequently _____ many of my teachers give _____. When class starts, they tell the students to close our books since we're going to take a quick test. Because _____ the material, I almost always get perfect scores on these tests _____ other students get poor grades.

Review the Material All at One Time

_____, simply reviewing the material all at one time is _____. I study this way for two simple reasons. The first is that I have an _____, so I only need to review the material once to remember it. When I take a test _____ going over the material, I can always remember everything I studied, and that lets me get _____. The second reason is that I'm very busy, so I _____ to study regularly. I play sports, do some _____, and help my parents at their restaurant after school ends. Because of my busy schedule, the only time I have _____ review the material is the night before a test.

B | Think about the following questions. Use your answers to them to help you organize your thoughts.

Review the Material Regularly

❶ Why do you like to review material regularly?
❷ How can reviewing material regularly benefit you?
❸ What happens to students who don't review material regularly?

Review the Material All at One Time

❶ Why do you like to review material at one time?
❷ How are you able to remember all the material if you review it at one time?
❸ What prevents you from reviewing material more regularly?

C | Now, write an outline of your response based on the answers that you gave to the questions on the previous page.

Your Choice _____

First Reason _____

Details _____

_____

Second Reason _____

Details _____

_____

D | Using the information in the outline above, write your response here.

_____

_____

_____

_____

_____

_____

_____

_____

_____

_____

_____

E | Now, say your response out loud to your partner. Don't look at your writing while you speak.

🎧 Q1_05_3

Do you agree or disagree with the following statement?

It is better to speak with a teacher than to talk to some other students in a class when you are having problems studying.

Please include specific examples and details to support your explanation.

PREPARATION TIME
00:00:15

RESPONSE TIME
00:00:45

Question Which would you prefer, having a job that requires you to use a computer and other types of modern technology or working at a place where you do not have to use them? Please include specific examples and details to support your explanation.

A | Listen to the following sample responses. Fill in the blanks as you listen. 🎧 Q1_06_1 / Q1_06_2

Have To

When I get a job in the future, I _____ have to use a computer and other types of modern technology. I enjoy using computers and am _____. For me, using a computer is fun, _____ a job in which I get to use a computer would be one I'd enjoy. I'm also _____ technology because I hope to become an engineer in the future. I expect that I'll _____ use a computer _____ use other various type of modern technology when I find employment as an engineer. _____, for me to accomplish my goal of becoming an engineer, I must _____ all kinds of modern technology.

Do Not Have To

_____ many people love computers and modern technology, I'm _____, so I'd prefer to have a job in which I _____ use them. I occasionally use my computer to surf the Internet, but I'm _____ working with it. It takes me a long time to do what I want, so _____ have to deal with computers when I get a job. _____, I want an outdoor job, not an office job. If I'm _____, then I simply won't be able to use a computer to do my duties. Thus if I get the kind of job I hope to have, I _____ use a computer.

B | Think about the following questions. Use your answers to them to help you organize your thoughts.

Have To

1. What do you want to do in the future?
2. How will that job require you to use a computer or modern technology?
3. How comfortable are you with computers and modern technology?

Do Not Have To

1. What do you want to do in the future?
2. Why won't you have to use a computer or modern technology to do that job?
3. Will your ability to do your job be hurt if you don't use a computer or modern technology?

C   Now, write an outline of your response based on the answers that you gave to the questions on the previous page.

Your Choice _____

First Reason _____

Details _____

_____

Second Reason _____

Details _____

_____

D   Using the information in the outline above, write your response here.

_____

_____

_____

_____

_____

_____

_____

_____

_____

_____

E   Now, say your response out loud to your partner. Don't look at your writing while you speak.

iBT Practice Test

VOLUME HELP NEXT

Q1_06_3

Which do you prefer, shopping at a big grocery store or a small one? Please include specific examples and details to support your explanation.

PREPARATION TIME
00:00:15

RESPONSE TIME
00:00:45

Question Answer one of the following questions.

1 Some people prefer doing the same task again and again while others prefer to do a variety of tasks. Talk about the advantages and disadvantages of doing the same task again and again. Use details and examples to explain your answer.

2 Some people prefer doing the same task again and again while others prefer to do a variety of tasks. Talk about the advantages and disadvantages of doing a variety of tasks. Use details and examples to explain your answer.

A | **Listen to the following sample responses. Fill in the blanks as you listen.** 🎧 Q1_07_1 / Q1_07_2

Doing the Same Tasks Again and Again

I can think of _____ to doing the same task again and again. The most _____ one is that a person can become very _____ that task. My older brother works on an _____ in a factory and does _____ each and every day. As a result, he has become _____ his job. Another advantage is that when a person does the same task _____, that individual can think about other things because doing the task doesn't _____. A major disadvantage is that a person can get _____ easily. My brother _____ about his job all the time because it's _____ exciting _____ interesting. He often says that he wishes he could do _____.

Doing a Variety of Tasks

One of the advantages of doing a variety of tasks is that they will _____. In other words, a person won't _____ by doing the same thing repeatedly. A second advantage is that a person can develop _____. My uncle does several tasks at his job, and he has _____ because of his abilities. As for _____, doing too many tasks can make it hard for some people to become _____ any of them. In addition, some people might get _____ by having to do too many activities. _____, my cousin works at a clothing store. She has to help customers, run the _____, put clothes on racks, and do other tasks. She hates _____ so many different tasks.

B | **Think about the following questions. Use your answers to them to help you organize your thoughts.**

Doing the Same Tasks Again and Again

1. How can doing the same task again and again benefit people?
2. What problems can doing the same task again and again cause?

Doing a Variety of Tasks

1. How can doing a variety of tasks help people?
2. What are some problems that doing a variety of tasks can cause?

C | **Now, write an outline of your response based on the answers that you gave to the questions above.**

Topic Sentence

First Reason

Details

Second Reason

Details

D | **Using the information in the outline above, write your response here.**

E | **Now, say your response out loud to your partner. Don't look at your writing while you speak.**

iBT Practice Test

🎧 Q1_07_3

Answer one of the following questions.

1 Some people prefer to work for themselves while others prefer to work for a company. Talk about the advantages and disadvantages of working for yourself. Use details and examples to explain your answer.

2 Some people prefer to work for themselves while others prefer to work for a company. Talk about the advantages and disadvantages of working for a company. Use details and examples to explain your answer.

PREPARATION TIME
00:00:15

RESPONSE TIME
00:00:45

Question A local resident has donated some land to the city. How should the city use the land?

• By making a flower garden

• By constructing a children's playground

• By selling it to a company that will develop the land

Use details and examples to explain your answer.

A Listen to the following sample responses. Fill in the blanks as you listen. 🎧 Q1_08_1 / Q1_08_2

Making a Flower Garden

_____, the city should make a flower garden. _____, my city doesn't have enough _____. There are only a couple of parks, but they are _____. A flower garden would add an _____ green space to the city. That would _____ the neighborhood it's in and be good for the _____, too. Secondly, there are few places of _____ in my city for people to visit. A flower garden would be such a wonderful place for people to _____ and to enjoy. I know I would love to go there, and _____ other people would also like to do that. It would be a great place to _____, to think, and just to enjoy the _____.

Constructing a Children's Playground

I like all three choices, _____, the best one is to construct a children's playground. There are _____ places for children to play in my city. If the city _____ construct a playground, many children _____ go there and have fun after school and on the weekend. I have a _____, and he would love a place like that. He could have fun and meet some new kids to play with. _____, these days, too many kids stay indoors and never _____. But if the city built a new playground, more kids might _____. Getting exercise could improve their health and keep them from becoming _____ and out of shape.

B Think about the following questions. Use your answers to them to help you organize your thoughts.

Making a Flower Garden

① How would a flower garden help local residents?

② Who would enjoy visiting a flower garden?

Constructing a Children's Playground

① Who would be happy about a children's playground?

② What are some benefits of a playground?

Selling It to a Company That Will Develop the Land

① What kind of development could the company do?

② What benefits would that development provide for the city and its residents?

C | **Now, write an outline of your response based on the answers that you gave to the questions above.**

Topic Sentence _____

First Reason _____

Details _____

_____

Second Reason _____

Details _____

_____

D | **Using the information in the outline above, write your response here.**

_____

_____

_____

_____

_____

_____

_____

_____

E | **Now, say your response out loud to your partner. Don't look at your writing while you speak.**

iBT Practice Test

🎧 Q1_08_3

Answer one of the following questions.

1　Some people believe that children should learn to be independent at a young age while others believe that children can learn independence later in life. Talk about the advantages and disadvantages of learning to be independent at a young age. Use details and examples to explain your answer.

2　Some people believe that children should learn to be independent at a young age while others believe that children can learn independence later in life. Talk about the advantages and disadvantages of learning to be independent later in life. Use details and examples to explain your answer.

PREPARATION TIME
00:00:15

RESPONSE TIME
00:00:45

A ┃ **Listen to the following sample responses. Fill in the blanks as you listen.** 🎧 Q1_09_1 / Q1_09_2

Agree

I _____ agree with the statement. I believe it's _____ for teachers to give feedback directly to their students. First of all, students can ask teachers questions and get _____ when they don't understand something. For example, my teacher gave me some feedback on a _____ I wrote, but I wasn't sure _____ what he meant. Since we were talking at the time, I asked him to _____, and he did that. Then, I knew exactly what he wanted me to do. _____ is that students and teachers can sometimes have good _____ when giving and receiving feedback. In the past, I've received feedback from teachers _____ led to us talking about topics that were interesting. I enjoyed those conversations and _____ them.

Disagree

I _____ that teachers should always give feedback directly to their students. _____, written feedback is fine. Most of my teachers write _____ on papers and tests. They explain what they want me to do, and I do it. I _____ speak with them in person to understand what they want. Plus, I can _____ written feedback anytime, so I won't _____ it. Something else to _____ is that most teachers are really busy. They _____ don't have time to speak with every student for five or ten minutes to _____. They'd never have time for class if they did that. I _____ when teachers talk to me, but I don't believe it's _____ or _____ to give every student personalized attention.

B ┃ **Think about the following questions. Use your answers to them to help you organize your thoughts.**

Agree

❶ How can students benefit from face-to-face feedback?

Disagree

❶ Why is it not necessary to get feedback directly from teachers?

❷ What is your personal experience with direct feedback from teachers?

❷ What other kinds of feedback can benefit students?

C | **Now, write an outline of your response based on the answers that you gave to the questions above.**

Your Choice _____

First Reason _____

Details _____

_____

Second Reason _____

Details _____

_____

D | **Using the information in the outline above, write your response here.**

_____

_____

_____

_____

_____

_____

_____

_____

_____

E | **Now, say your response out loud to your partner. Don't look at your writing while you speak.**

iBT Practice Test

🎧 Q1_09_3

Do you agree or disagree with the following statement?

Schools no longer need to teach math to students because there have been many technological advances in recent years.

Use details and examples to explain your answer.

PREPARATION TIME
00:00:15

RESPONSE TIME
00:00:45

Question Do you agree or disagree with the following statement?

All students should spend at least one semester studying in another country.

Use details and examples to explain your answer.

A | **Listen to the following sample responses. Fill in the blanks as you listen.** 🎧 Q1_10_1 / Q1_10_2

Agree

I _____ all students should spend at least one semester studying in another country. For one thing, they can have the _____ to learn a new language and culture. My cousin studied _____ in Italy and learned Italian. She can speak it _____ now. She also knows about Italian culture _____ her semester abroad. Another _____ is that students have the opportunity to see how other people live. We often _____ that everyone is similar to each other, but that's not true. My cousin was _____ by how different her Italian host family was from her own family. It was a _____ for her to realize that not everybody does the same _____, eats the same foods, or has the same _____.

Disagree

I _____ with the statement for two reasons. The first reason is that studying abroad is _____, and large numbers of families cannot _____ it. One of my friends studied abroad for a semester. His family _____ so that he could go abroad, and it was hard for them to _____. He never should have studied abroad. The second reason is that most people will _____ in their lives. They will always remain in their own country. It's therefore _____ for most people to study in other lands since _____ doing that is to learn a new language and culture. Because most people won't ever travel abroad, they _____ learn about foreign countries or experience them.

B | **Think about the following questions. Use your answers to them to help you organize your thoughts.**

Agree

❶ Why should students spend a semester studying abroad?

Disagree

❶ How can studying abroad be harmful or cause problems for students?

② What benefits can students get from studying abroad?

② Why is it unnecessary for students to study abroad?

C **Now, write an outline of your response based on the answers that you gave to the questions above.**

Topic Sentence _____

First Reason _____

Details _____

_____

Second Reason _____

Details _____

_____

D **Using the information in the outline above, write your response here.**

_____

_____

_____

_____

_____

_____

_____

_____

_____

E **Now, say your response out loud to your partner. Don't look at your writing while you speak.**

iBT Practice Test

Q1_10_3

Do you agree or disagree with the following statement?

Students should be taught how to be healthy at school.

Use details and examples to explain your answer.

PREPARATION TIME
00:00:15

RESPONSE TIME
00:00:45

Part **B**

Integrated Speaking Tasks
Reading, Listening, and Speaking

Questions 2 & 3

Integrated Speaking Tasks | Reading, Listening, and Speaking

◢ About the Tasks

The second and third questions require you to integrate different language skills. First, you are presented with a short reading passage and are given 45 or 50 seconds to read it. After that, you will listen to a conversation or a lecture related to the information presented in the reading passage. Then, you need to organize your response by using information from both the reading passage and the conversation or lecture. For these questions, you are given 30 seconds to prepare your response and 60 seconds to speak.

Question 2 concerns a topic of campus-related interest but requires no prior firsthand experience of college or university life in North America to understand the topic. The reading passage is usually between 75 and 100 words long. It may be an announcement, letter, or article regarding a policy, rule, or future plan of a college or university. It may also be related to campus facilities or the quality of life on campus. After reading the passage, you will listen to two speakers discuss the topic presented in the reading passage. Typically, one of the two speakers shows a strong opinion about the topic. You need to summarize the speaker's opinion and the reasons the speaker holds it.

In **Question 3**, you will read a short passage about an academic subject and then listen to a professor lecture about that subject. The question requires you to relate the reading passage and the lecture. Topics for this question can be drawn from a variety of fields, including life science, social science, physical science, and the humanities. However, the question does not require prior knowledge of any particular field.

When you answer the questions, be sure to use only the information that is presented in the reading passage and conversation or lecture. Even if you possess outside knowledge of the topic, you should not use it. In addition, when listening to the speakers, focus specifically on the one who is expressing a strong opinion about the topic. Ignore whatever the other person says. As for the professor, pay close attention to the examples he or she gives and then use them to show how the lecture is related to the reading passage.

⌒ Q2_00_1

Library to Sell Unused Books

The library at City University intends to sell a large number of its unused books. Books are considered unused if they have not been checked out once in the past five years. The library estimates that it possesses more than 5,000 unused books but only plans to sell between 1,500 and 2,000 of them. All proceeds from the sales of unused books will go toward the purchase of new books or reference materials. The shelf space gained from the sales of unused books will be utilized for the library's expanding reference section.

The man expresses his opinion about the announcement by the school library. Explain his opinion and the reasons he gives for holding that opinion.

PREPARATION TIME
00:00:30

RESPONSE TIME
00:00:60

Now listen to two students discussing the announcement.

M Student: Did you see that the library is going to be selling some books?

W Student: Yeah, I can't wait since I'm into collecting old books. I bet I can get some good ones.

M: Well, you might be excited, but I'm not.

W: Really?

M: The library should be obtaining more books, not getting rid of them. Just because a book hasn't been checked out doesn't mean that students aren't using it.

W: How is that possible?

M: I often take books from the shelves, photocopy the relevant pages, and then put them back on the shelves. Although I don't check them out, I still use them.

W: Hmm . . . I'd never considered something like that.

M: In addition, while nobody might have used a book in a while, students that attend school here in the future might. Many library books are on obscure topics that few people study, but they're still important. Imagine not being able to do some research because the library sold a book you wanted.

W: When you put it that way, maybe this book sale is a bad idea.

According to the announcement, the school library has several thousand books which it considers unused. It is planning to sell around 2,000 of these books in order to raise funds which can be used to buy new material and to create more space for its reference section. The man tells the woman that he is opposed to the decision to sell these books. He first states that even though students might not check out books, they are still using them. He remarks that he often gets books from the library and photocopies pages in them. However, he never borrows any of those books, so they erroneously appear to be unused. He also comments that future students might need some books that are currently unused, yet if the library sells those books, they won't be able to do the research that they need to do.

🎧 Q3_00_1

The Mere-Exposure Effect

When people are exposed to a new stimulus, they tend to dislike it, to feel uncomfortable around it, or to want to avoid it. However, as they become more exposed to the stimulus, their attitude typically changes, and they come to like it more. This is known as the mere-exposure effect, which is also called the familiarity effect. Essentially, familiarity results in people developing a liking for something. Stimuli that can result in the mere-exposure effect taking place can be people, sounds, tastes, and places, among others.

The professor talks about her personal experiences. Explain how they are related to the mere-exposure effect.

PREPARATION TIME
00:00:30

RESPONSE TIME
00:00:60

Now listen to a lecture on this topic in a psychology class.

W Professor: We've all heard that familiarity breeds contempt. Well, uh, that's not exactly true, and I'd say that as a general rule, the more exposed we are to something, the more we come to like it. Let me give you a couple of examples . . . Hmm . . . My husband loves country music, but when I first heard him listening to it, I hated the music so much that it drove me crazy. But we've been married for twelve years, so over time, I've gotten used to country music. In fact, I've recently found myself listening to the country music radio station while driving. As I've been exposed to it, I've come to appreciate it.

Here's another one . . . There's a coffee shop I visit every morning before coming to work. About a year ago, a new customer started showing up at around the same time as me. At first, I was suspicious of him and thought he might be following me. However, the more I've seen him, the less I dislike him. Now, uh, I've never had a conversation with him, but while I used to ignore him and he ignored me, now we always greet each other by waving or smiling when we're there at the same time. So I'd say that over time, we've both succumbed to the familiarity effect.

Q3_00_2

The professor gives two examples from her personal life to show how her attitude has changed over time. The first regards her husband. She comments that he listens to country music, which she hated when she first heard it. However, she has been married for more than a decade, so she has gotten used to country music and sometimes even willingly listens to it. The second example she gives is of a man in a coffee shop. She was suspicious of him because he was often there when she was, so she disliked him. But as time passed, she has become more familiar with him and now greets him with a wave and a smile. Both stories are examples of the mere-exposure effect. According to it, when people are exposed to something new, they often dislike it, but as they get used to it, they come to like it.

A   Read the following letter to the editor in the school newspaper. Try to understand what the letter is about. After reading the letter, complete the notes below.

Problems with Dormitory Room Assignments

I am a freshman and have a serious problem with how the university handles its room assignments in dormitories for incoming students. I failed to receive any information at all about my roommate, which resulted in several problems. Once the school makes room assignments, it should provide every student with the name and the email address of his or her future roommate. That will enable the roommates to communicate to find out what items they will bring and whether they have enough in common that they will be able to get along well. Doing so will avert many future problems.

Eric Thompson
Freshman

What the Student Suggests _____

Details _____

_____

_____

_____

B   Listen to a conversation about the same topic. Be sure to take notes while you listen.

🎧 Q2_01_1

Man's Opinion _____

First Reason _____

Details _____

_____

Second Reason _____

Details _____

_____

C Read the question and write your response by using the information in your notes.

Question The man expresses his opinion about the letter to the editor in the school newspaper. Explain his opinion and the reasons he gives for holding that opinion.

D Now, say your response out loud to your partner. Don't look at your writing while you speak.

iBT Practice Test

Question 2 of 4

VOLUME

HELP

NEXT

READING TIME 00:00:45

🎧 Q2_01_3

Textbooks Too Expensive

I am tired of paying excessively high prices for my textbooks. I am majoring in English Literature, so many of my classes require me to purchase five or more textbooks. I regularly spend more than $400 a semester on books. Since I don't know what books are needed before the semester begins, I have to buy them at the school bookstore, which is expensive. The school should post a list of required books for each class prior to the start of the semester. This will permit students to purchase the materials at used bookstores or online for cheaper prices.

Rashid Randolph
Senior

The woman expresses her opinion about the letter to the editor in the school newspaper. Explain her opinion and the reasons she gives for holding that opinion.

PREPARATION TIME
00:00:30

RESPONSE TIME
00:00:60

A Read the following announcement by the Music Department. Try to understand what the announcement is about. After reading the announcement, complete the notes below.

Johann Gathers to Become Orchestra Director

As of tomorrow, Professor Johann Gathers of the Music Department will become the new director of the school orchestra. Dr. Gathers has been a professor in the Music Department for the past fifteen years and is well regarded by students, faculty, and staff members. He is replacing Carl Franks, who has resigned immediately due to personal reasons. Dr. Gathers stated that the upcoming concert by the school orchestra scheduled for September 22 will continue as planned. He intends to meet with the members of the orchestra to speak with them soon.

What Will Happen _____

Details _____

_____

_____

B Listen to a conversation about the same topic. Be sure to take notes while you listen.

🎧 Q2_02_1

Man's Opinion _____

First Reason _____

Details _____

_____

Second Reason _____

Details _____

C | Read the question and write your response by using the information in your notes.

Question The man expresses his opinion about the announcement by the Music Department. Explain his opinion and the reasons he gives for holding that opinion.

D | Now, say your response out loud to your partner. Don't look at your writing while you speak.

◠ Q2_02_3

Stop Selling Junk Food

There is a severe health epidemic on campus, and the university is making it worse. I have noticed that many students—easily greater than half of the student body—are overweight and out of shape. But the university persists in selling junk food such as sodas and candy in the stores and cafés located on campus. These unhealthy foods have no nutritional value and should not be sold to students. I strongly urge the school immediately to cease the selling of these items everywhere on campus.

Susan Moriarty
Sophomore

The woman expresses her opinion about the letter to the editor in the school newspaper. Explain her opinion and the reasons she gives for holding that opinion.

PREPARATION TIME
00:00:30

RESPONSE TIME
00:00:60

A Read the following announcement by the student services office. Try to understand what the announcement is about. After reading the announcement, complete the notes below.

Rental Car Agency to Open on Campus

The student services office is going to begin renting cars to students who are enrolled full time. This service is set to begin on January 14 when the spring semester starts. There will be a wide variety of cars to choose from. The rates for the cars will be comparable to those charged by leading national rental car agencies. To be eligible to rent a car, students must have a valid driver's license from their state of residence and a GPA of 2.50 or higher. For more details, please contact the student services office at extension 5094.

What Students Need to Do _____

Details _____

_____

_____

_____

_____

B Listen to a conversation about the same topic. Be sure to take notes while you listen.

🎧 Q2_03_1

Man's Opinion _____

First Reason _____

Details _____

_____

Second Reason _____

Details _____

_____

C | **Read the question and write your response by using the information in your notes.**

Question The man expresses his opinion about the announcement by the student services office. Explain his opinion and the reasons he gives for holding that opinion.

_____

_____

_____

_____

_____

_____

_____

_____

_____

D | **Now, say your response out loud to your partner. Don't look at your writing while you speak.**

🎧 Q2_03_3

Faculty Parking Lot Now Open to Students

The faculty parking lot located between Emerson Hall and Branson Hall will be open to students with parking stickers as of Monday, September 2. There are 130 parking spots in the lot. However, students will not be allowed to park in every spot in the lot. Those spaces specifically reserved for faculty will be marked both with signs and blue paint in the spots themselves. Students who park in reserved spots will receive parking fines of $75. For more information, visit the transportation office at 43 Miller Avenue.

The woman expresses her opinion about the announcement by the transportation office. Explain her opinion and the reasons she gives for holding that opinion.

PREPARATION TIME
00:00:30

RESPONSE TIME
00:00:60

A | **Read the following announcement by the Math Department. Try to understand what the announcement is about. After reading the announcement, complete the notes below.**

Online Math Tutoring Available

On account of high demand, online tutoring in math will be made available starting on October 2. All tutoring will be conducted by graduate students in the Math Department or junior or senior Math majors with a minimum GPA of 3.30. Students can arrange tutorial sessions by calling 831-1945 or by visiting the Math Department in room 402 in Richardson Hall. Students will be charged based upon the number of hours of tutoring they require and the times when they wish to have their tutoring sessions.

What Will Happen _____

Details _____

B | **Listen to a conversation about the same topic. Be sure to take notes while you listen.**
🎧 Q2_04_1

Woman's Opinion _____

First Reason _____

Details _____

Second Reason _____

Details _____

C | Read the question and write your response by using the information in your notes.

> Question The woman expresses her opinion about the announcement by the Math Department. Explain her opinion and the reasons she gives for holding that opinion.

D | Now, say your response out loud to your partner. Don't look at your writing while you speak.

🎧 Q2_04_3

Engineering Group Study Sessions to End

The weekly engineering group study sessions for freshmen will not be held during the spring semester. The sessions are being canceled due to a lack of interest by this year's freshmen class as well as the inability to find tutors willing to lead the sessions. Those individuals who wish to receive extra assistance in their engineering classes may either form their own study groups or hire tutors from the tutoring center. The number of the tutoring center is 584-5494. Any questions regarding the study sessions should be directed to the office of the dean of engineering.

The man expresses his opinion about the announcement by the dean of engineering. Explain his opinion and the reasons he gives for holding that opinion.

PREPARATION TIME
00:00:30

RESPONSE TIME
00:00:60

A **Read the following announcement by the student activities office. Try to understand what the announcement is about. After reading the announcement, complete the notes below.**

Hiking Club to Open

The student services office has decided to permit a new club to be established. It will be called the hiking club and will be open to all full-time and part-time students interested in hiking. Meeting times for the club have yet to be determined, but club members will go on hikes in the surrounding area several times per semester. The first meeting of the club will be on Monday, September 2, at 6:00 P.M. It will be held in room 435 in Carter Hall. The club's officers will be elected at the meeting.

What Will Happen _____

Details _____

_____

_____

B **Listen to a conversation about the same topic. Be sure to take notes while you listen.**

🎧 Q2_05_1

Man's Opinion _____

First Reason _____

Details _____

_____

Second Reason _____

Details _____

_____

C Read the question and write your response by using the information in your notes.

Question The man expresses his opinion about the announcement by the student activities office. Explain his opinion and the reasons he gives for holding that opinion.

_____

_____

_____

_____

_____

_____

_____

_____

_____

_____

D Now, say your response out loud to your partner. Don't look at your writing while you speak.

iBT Practice Test

Question 2 of 4

VOLUME

HELP

NEXT

READING TIME 00:00:45

🎧 Q2_05_3

Archaeology Seminars to Expand Enrollment

The faculty in the Archaeology Department have unanimously decided to expand the enrollment for the seminars being given in the fall and spring semesters this academic year. There are two seminars scheduled for each semester. Normal enrollment is fifteen students, but up to twenty-five students will be permitted to take the seminars, which are required for Archaeology majors to graduate. In recent years, the number of Archaeology majors has increased dramatically, which has necessitated this change. Please visit the Archaeology Department office in Jones Hall for a schedule of this semester's seminars.

The woman expresses her opinion about the announcement by the Archaeology Department. Explain her opinion and the reasons she gives for holding that opinion.

PREPARATION TIME
00:00:30

RESPONSE TIME
00:00:60

A | **Read the following announcement by the Registrar's office. Try to understand what the announcement is about. After reading the announcement, complete the notes below.**

All Summer Classes Canceled

All classes in the college of arts and sciences and the college of business that were scheduled to be held during the summer session have been canceled. This refers to classes supposed to take place in both the first and second summer sessions. There has not been sufficient interest in summer classes this year as only 5% of all possible seats in the scheduled classes have been filled. That is not enough to warrant teaching any classes this summer. Please call the Registrar's office at 890-3481 if you have any questions or comments.

What Will Happen _____

Details _____

_____

_____

B | **Listen to a conversation about the same topic. Be sure to take notes while you listen.**
Q2_06_1

Man's Opinion _____

First Reason _____

Details _____

_____

Second Reason _____

Details _____

_____

C | Read the question and write your response by using the information in your notes.

Question The man expresses his opinion about the announcement by the Registrar's office. Explain his opinion and the reasons he gives for holding that opinion.

_____

_____

_____

_____

_____

_____

_____

_____

_____

D | Now, say your response out loud to your partner. Don't look at your writing while you speak.

iBT Practice Test

VOLUME

HELP

NEXT

Question 2 of 4

READING TIME 00:00:45

🎧 Q2_06_3

Changes in School Athletics

Once the City University men's and women's basketball teams end their seasons, both teams will be disbanded. This is the last year for the foreseeable future that the school will have organized men's and women's basketball teams. The school is facing a severe financial crisis, and neither team is able to pay for itself through the sales of tickets and concessions. As a result, the school cannot afford to pay for either team. Those players who have scholarships may keep them until they graduate or may transfer elsewhere to continue playing basketball.

The woman expresses her opinion about the announcement by the dean of students. Explain her opinion and the reasons she gives for holding that opinion.

PREPARATION TIME
00:00:30

RESPONSE TIME
00:00:60

A Read the following announcement by the university student housing office. Try to understand what the announcement is about. After reading the announcement, complete the notes below.

Freshman-Only Dormitories Available

Starting during the fall semester, freshman-only dormitories will be available on campus. Both Robinson Hall and Dixon Hall will no longer house upperclassmen. Instead, they will be reserved only for freshmen. There will be single and double rooms available in each dormitory. The resident assistants on each floor will also serve as tutors in various subjects. They will be able to provide free academic instruction for students living in the dormitories. To apply for a room in one of the dormitories, please contact the housing office at 545-9820.

What Will Happen _____

Details _____

_____

_____

_____

B Listen to a conversation about the same topic. Be sure to take notes while you listen.

🎧 Q2_07_1

Man's Opinion _____

First Reason _____

Details _____

_____

Second Reason _____

Details _____

_____

C | Read the question and write your response by using the information in your notes.

> Question The man expresses his opinion about the announcement by the university student housing office. Explain his opinion and the reasons he gives for holding that opinion.

D | Now, say your response out loud to your partner. Don't look at your writing while you speak.

iBT Practice Test

Question 2 of 4

VOLUME

HELP

NEXT

READING TIME 00:00:45

🎧 Q2_07_3

Library to Hold Information Sessions

In recent years, many of the library's holdings have gone online. This includes newspapers, journals, and reference materials. In an effort to make accessing these holdings easier, the library will be holding several information sessions for two weeks. From Monday, January 16, until Friday, January 27, the library will hold two information sessions each day, including on Saturday and Sunday. The sessions will be from 10:00 AM to 11:00 AM and from 6:00 PM to 7:00 PM. There is room for thirty students in each session. Seats are available on a first-come, first-served basis.

The woman expresses her opinion about the announcement by the university library. Explain her opinion and the reasons she gives for holding that opinion.

PREPARATION TIME
00:00:30

RESPONSE TIME
00:00:60

A Read the following advertisement by the university study abroad office. Try to understand what the advertisement is about. After reading the advertisement, complete the notes below.

Come to the Lunch and Learn Program

This Thursday at 1:00 PM, the study abroad office is sponsoring the Lunch and Learn Program. Enjoy a special catered lunch at the office and learn about various opportunities that exist to study abroad. The lunch will feature foods from countries around the world. You will have the opportunity to sample food you might get to eat daily if you study in another country. You can also speak with some students who studied abroad in the past. And you can hear a talk by Andrea Carrano, the director of the study abroad program. Call 323-4847 for more information.

What Will Happen _____

Details _____

B Listen to a conversation about the same topic. Be sure to take notes while you listen.

🎧 Q2_08_1

Man's Opinion _____

First Reason _____

Details _____

Second Reason _____

Details _____

C | Read the question and write your response by using the information in your notes.

Question The man expresses his opinion about the advertisement by the university study abroad office. Explain his opinion and the reasons he gives for holding that opinion.

D | Now, say your response out loud to your partner. Don't look at your writing while you speak.

iBT Practice Test

Question 2 of 4

VOLUME

HELP

NEXT

READING TIME 00:00:45

🎧 Q2_08_3

Scholarships for Volunteers

Thanks to a generous donation from an anonymous benefactor, the school will be presenting ten scholarships worth $2,000 each to students starting next semester. The scholarships will be awarded only to those students who participate in volunteer activities in the local community. To apply, a student must have a GPA of at least 3.20. A 500-word essay about how volunteering has affected the student's life must also be submitted. All submissions are due at the office of the dean of students no later than April 10.

The woman expresses her opinion about the announcement by the office of the dean of students. Explain her opinion and the reasons she gives for holding that opinion.

PREPARATION TIME
00:00:30

RESPONSE TIME
00:00:60

A Read the following notice by the Buildings and Grounds Department. Try to understand what the notice is about. After reading the notice, complete the notes below.

Thermostats to Be Centrally Controlled

This summer vacation, there will be changes in the heating and cooling systems in every building on campus. The heat and the air will no longer be able to be controlled in individual rooms. Instead, the thermostats in rooms will be removed, and the heating and air-conditioning systems will be centrally controlled by the Buildings and Grounds Department. This will prevent rooms from getting too hot or cold throughout the year. It will also save the university a considerable amount of money.

What Will Happen _____

Details _____

_____

_____

_____

B Listen to a conversation about the same topic. Be sure to take notes while you listen.
🎧 Q2_09_1

Man's Opinion _____

First Reason _____

Details _____

_____

Second Reason _____

Details _____

C | **Read the question and write your response by using the information in your notes.**

> Question The man expresses his opinion about the notice by the Buildings and Grounds Department. Explain his opinion and the reasons he gives for holding that opinion.

_____

_____

_____

_____

_____

_____

_____

_____

_____

_____

D | **Now, say your response out loud to your partner. Don't look at your writing while you speak.**

VOLUME　HELP　NEXT

READING TIME 00:00:45

Q2_09_3

Newspaper Issues to Cost Money

Starting on Monday, September 1, print issues of the *Central University Daily* will cost $0.25 each. Due to decreasing advertising rates and the increasing prices of paper, ink, and printing, the newspaper has been losing money for the past two years. It is our hope that we can stop losing money by charging for each issue. Interested individuals may subscribe to the newspaper as well. Contact Debbie Foster at 549-3392 for more information about pricing. Comments are always welcome. They may be submitted to the newspaper office at room 403 in Baker Hall.

The man expresses his opinion about the notice by the school newspaper. Explain his opinion and the reasons he gives for holding that opinion.

PREPARATION TIME
00:00:30

RESPONSE TIME
00:00:60

A | Read the following announcement by the Astronomy Department. Try to understand what the announcement is about. After reading the announcement, complete the notes below.

School to Build Observatory

Thanks to a generous grant from the Fullenwider Foundation, the school has obtained enough funding to construct an observatory on campus. The observatory will be constructed in the northwest corner of campus, where it is the darkest. It will contain a sixteen-inch refracting telescope as well as other advanced technology capable of observing the night sky. Some classes will be taught there, and it is expected that students and faculty will be able to reserve times to use the telescope. The observatory should be complete in one year.

What Will Happen _____

Details _____

_____

_____

B | Listen to a conversation about the same topic. Be sure to take notes while you listen.

🎧 Q2_10_1

Woman's Opinion _____

First Reason _____

Details _____

_____

Second Reason _____

Details _____

_____

C Read the question and write your response by using the information in your notes.

Question The woman expresses her opinion about the announcement by the Astronomy Department. Explain her opinion and the reasons she gives for holding that opinion.

D Now, say your response out loud to your partner. Don't look at your writing while you speak.

🎧 Q2_10_3

Library Should Fully Open Archives

I recently attempted to gain access to the university's archives in order to conduct some research on a project I am doing for a class. To my great disappointment, my request to read some of the founding documents of our university was denied. I was told by the librarian that only professors and some graduate students are permitted access to the archives. This is wrong. The library's archives should be open to all students, both undergraduates and graduates. Material in the library should be shared, not hoarded for a mere few to utilize.

Cynthia Desmond

Junior

The man expresses his opinion about the letter to the editor in the school newspaper. Explain his opinion and the reasons he gives for holding that opinion.

PREPARATION TIME
00:00:30

RESPONSE TIME
00:00:60

A Read the following passage. Try to understand what the passage is about. After reading the passage, complete the notes below.

Approach-Avoidance Behavior

In some instances, people may experience mixed feelings so that a situation may have both positive and negative aspects. The positive features attract people to the situation whereas the negative ones repel them. The simultaneous occurring of both positive and negative feelings causes a conflict in the person, which results in what is known as approach-avoidance behavior. When instances such as this occur, people may suffer from stress as they are unable to decide whether to approach a situation or to avoid it.

Main Idea of the Passage _____

Details _____

_____

_____

_____

_____

B Listen to a lecture about the same topic. Be sure to take notes while you listen. 🎧 Q3_01_1

Thesis Statement _____

Example _____

What the professor's friend expected _____

_____

What she learned afterward _____

_____

_____

C | Read the question and write your response by using the information in your notes.

Question The professor talks about his friend's interest in becoming a teacher. Explain how it is related to approach-avoidance behavior.

D | Now, say your response out loud to your partner. Don't look at your writing while you speak.

🎧 Q3_01_3

Sensitization

An animal may sometimes be exposed to an innocuous outside stimulus which is closely followed by an excessive shock. When this occurs, the animal may overreact in some manner. Then, the next time the same outside stimulus happens to the animal, it will have an exaggerated reaction on account of the shock that occurred in the previous situation. Despite the stimulus and the shock not being related, the animal associates them with each other and continues overreacting each time it is exposed to the stimulus.

The professor talks about the reactions of animals to various shocks. Explain how they are related to sensitization.

PREPARATION TIME
00:00:30

RESPONSE TIME
00:00:60

A Read the following passage. Try to understand what the passage is about. After reading the passage, complete the notes below.

Planning Fallacy

Planning future tasks frequently requires people to estimate how much time they require to complete them. In many cases, people make overly optimistic predictions regarding how much work they can complete in a given period of time, so they underestimate the time required. They additionally neglect to make allowances for unexpected problems. Therefore, they fail to complete their tasks before they are due on account of a lack of time. This phenomenon, termed planning fallacy, usually only occurs when dealing with one's own work as people tend to overestimate the amount of time needed for others to complete their tasks.

Main Idea of the Passage _____

Details _____

_____

_____

_____

_____

B Listen to a lecture about the same topic. Be sure to take notes while you listen. 🎧 Q3_02_1

Thesis Statement _____

Example _____

What the professor expected _____

_____

What actually happened _____

_____

C | **Read the question and write your response by using the information in your notes.**

Question The professor talks about one of his experiences when he was a student. Explain how it is related to planning fallacy.

D | **Now, say your response out loud to your partner. Don't look at your writing while you speak.**

🎧 Q3_02_3

Experience Goods

There are some products about which it is difficult for consumers to determine their quality until they are actually used. These are known as experience goods. Because consumers need to use them before deciding how good the items are, they are often wary of purchasing these products unless someone they trust guarantees the quality of the goods. Trusted individuals may be relatives and close friends, but they may also be celebrities known to have used the products or consumer agencies with good reputations.

The professor talks about his friend's experience selling a beauty cream. Explain how it is related to experience goods.

PREPARATION TIME
00:00:30

RESPONSE TIME
00:00:60

A Read the following passage. Try to understand what the passage is about. After reading the passage, complete the notes below.

Decision Making

Making decisions can be difficult, but, depending upon the nature of the choice, some are easier to make than others. When there is a matter of importance, arriving at a final decision tends to take a long time and may require a great deal of thought and planning. However, if the choice to be made is trivial, most people can do it quickly. In addition, the time and amount of effort required regularly depend on the decision maker's personality. Some people agonize over the simplest of choices whereas others find even crucial decisions easy to make.

Main Idea of the Passage _____

Details _____

_____

_____

_____

B Listen to a lecture about the same topic. Be sure to take notes while you listen. 🎧 Q3_03_1

Thesis Statement _____

First Example _____

Details _____

_____

Second Example _____

Details _____

_____

C | Read the question and write your response by using the information in your notes.

> Question The professor talks about some recent purchases he made. Explain how they are related to decision making.

_____

_____

_____

_____

_____

_____

_____

_____

_____

_____

D | Now, say your response out loud to your partner. Don't look at your writing while you speak.

Q3_03_3

Appeasement Behavior

When an animal acts in an aggressive manner toward another animal, typically one of its own species, the second animal may adopt a submissive stance in order to pacify the first one. This type of behavior is a survival strategy which is frequently utilized by weaker animals. Through the weaker animal's submissive behavior, it acknowledges the strength, power, and leadership of the aggressive animal and therefore avoids being attacked, which could result in serious injury or even death.

The professor talks about the actions of dogs and wolves. Explain how they are related to appeasement behavior.

PREPARATION TIME
00:00:30

RESPONSE TIME
00:00:60

A Read the following passage. Try to understand what the passage is about. After reading the passage, complete the notes below.

The Pratfall Effect

In movies and stage shows, a pratfall is a mistake done by a performer that has a comedic effect. This mistake makes the character more likeable to the audience. This carries over into everyday life. People who err are usually liked because they make others laugh while simultaneously appearing to be more human. They are in opposition to individuals who make no mistakes, resulting in them appearing to have cold or distant personalities and therefore being less likeable. These people are also more intimidating than individuals who make mistakes since they appear less threatening because of their errors.

Main Idea of the Passage _____

_____

Details _____

_____

B Listen to a lecture about the same topic. Be sure to take notes while you listen. 🎧 Q3_04_1

Thesis Statement _____

Example _____

What the first man did _____

What the second man did _____

People's responses _____

_____

_____

C   **Read the question and write your response by using the information in your notes.**

Question The professor talks about a study that was conducted. Explain how it is related to the pratfall effect.

_____

_____

_____

_____

_____

_____

_____

_____

_____

_____

_____

D   **Now, say your response out loud to your partner. Don't look at your writing while you speak.**

🎧 Q3_04_3

Market Fragmentation

The market for a product or service tends to change over time. One way it becomes different is through market fragmentation. This happens when a market that is homogenous in makeup fragments into multiple smaller segments. These segments have their own features, which may be rather different from the original form of the market. This process often results in various drawbacks to companies, the main one of which is the reduced effectiveness of previously successful mass-market techniques. There is additionally a loss of brand loyalty as new brands emerge to compete for customers.

The professor talks about changes in the American television market. Explain how they are related to market fragmentation.

PREPARATION TIME
00:00:30

RESPONSE TIME
00:00:60

A   Read the following passage. Try to understand what the passage is about. After reading the passage, complete the notes below.

Coevolution

Species evolve in various ways, and while doing so, they sometimes influence the evolution of other species through the process called coevolution. This takes place when one species relies upon another and that species in turn depends upon the first species for something else. In such cases, a reciprocal evolutionary process takes place. An evolutionary change in the morphology of one species precipitates a change in the second one. Coevolution can occur when species have a predator-prey or parasite-host relationship as well as when there is a mutualistic relationship between the two.

Main Idea of the Passage _____

Details _____

_____

_____

_____

B   Listen to a lecture about the same topic. Be sure to take notes while you listen. 🎧 Q3_05_1

Thesis Statement _____

First Example _____

Details _____

_____

Second Example _____

Details _____

_____

C | Read the question and write your response by using the information in your notes.

Question The professor talks about the relationships between certain organisms. Explain how they are related to coevolution.

D | Now, say your response out loud to your partner. Don't look at your writing while you speak.

Q3_05_3

Territoriality

Most animals jealously guard the area which they consider to be their territory. The region they occupy provides both food and shelter for them, and they also raise their offspring in this area. Many animals mark their territory, typically by leaving their scent at its borders. Intrusions by another animal of the same species may be swiftly met with aggressive posturing intended to scare off the invader. Should that fail, the animal defending its territory may physically attack or even kill the intruder.

The professor talks about the behavior of lions and European robins. Explain how it is related to territoriality.

PREPARATION TIME

00:00:30

RESPONSE TIME

00:00:60

A Read the following passage. Try to understand what the passage is about. After reading the passage, complete the notes below.

Role-Playing

Some individuals attempt to learn by taking part in simulated scenarios in which they pretend to have specific roles or occupations. For instance, in one situation, a person may pretend to be a doctor while others may act as if they are patients or nurses. The objective of this role-playing is for every participant to gain practical experience. Each person learns how to behave or what to do when confronted with a certain situation. Therefore, when something similar happens in reality in the future, the participants will know precisely how to act.

Main Idea of the Passage _____

Details _____

_____

_____

_____

_____

B Listen to a lecture about the same topic. Be sure to take notes while you listen. 🎧 Q3_06_1

Thesis Statement _____

Example _____

What the new employees did _____

_____

_____

How the feedback was helpful _____

_____

_____

C | Read the question and write your response by using the information in your notes.

> Question The professor talks about her experience working at a department store. Explain how it is related to role-playing.

D | Now, say your response out loud to your partner. Don't look at your writing while you speak.

iBT Practice Test

🎧 Q3_06_3

Passive Candidate Recruitment

The vast majority of the eligible workforce is already employed and not actively seeking to change employers. Hence many companies search for new employees through passive candidate recruitment. A passive candidate is a person who is not actively looking for another position but who can be enticed to change jobs. Companies often find these candidates through referrals from current employees or by advertising on Internet job boards. To entice passive candidates to change jobs, companies must offer them more attractive employment packages, including higher salaries, more vacation time, promotions, and housing, than they are presently receiving.

The professor talks about the experiences of two of his former classmates. Explain how they are related to passive candidate recruitment.

PREPARATION TIME
00:00:30

RESPONSE TIME
00:00:60

A | Read the following passage. Try to understand what the passage is about. After reading the passage, complete the notes below.

Erosion

The wearing away of soil is erosion. There are a variety of causes of it, but the most prominent of them is the removal of vegetation from the ground. Without plant roots in the ground, the soil can become loose. This lets it be more easily removed by forces such as wind and water. Erosion also occurs when rock and soil underground become unstable due to the creation of tunnel systems. They loosen the topsoil, allowing the wind and the water to remove it.

Main Idea of the Passage _____

Details _____

_____

_____

_____

B | Listen to part of a lecture about the same topic. Be sure to take notes while you listen.
🎧 Q3_07_1

Thesis Statement _____

First Example _____

Details _____

_____

_____

Second Example _____

Details _____

_____

C | Read the question and write your response by using the information in your notes.

Question The professor talks about grazing animals and muskrats. Explain how their actions are related to erosion.

_____

_____

_____

_____

_____

_____

_____

_____

_____

D | Now, say your response out loud to your partner. Don't look at your writing while you speak.

🎧 Q3_07_3

Echolocation

Echolocation is a type of biological sonar which is utilized by some animals. The animals emit high-pitched soundwaves in various directions and then listen for the echo to return. This lets the animals know what is all around them. Echolocation can be used to identify obstacles blocking an animal's way as well as prey to be hunted and predators to be avoided. In the animal kingdom, bats are the best-known animals that use echolocation. They employ it while hunting insects. In the oceans, whales and dolphins utilize echolocation for various purposes.

The professor talks about crickets and praying mantises. Explain how their actions are related to echolocation.

PREPARATION TIME
00:00:30

RESPONSE TIME
00:00:60

A   **Read the following passage. Try to understand what the passage is about. After reading the passage, complete the notes below.**

Tonic Immobility

Tonic immobility is the scientific term for when animals play dead. When animals pretend to be dead, their bodies go limp, and they typically roll over onto their sides or backs. Some animals playing dead stick out their tongues while some, such as the opossum, empty their bowels and excrete a foul-smelling substance to convince other animals that they really are dead. These animals do not respond when they are poked, prodded, or even picked up by other animals. A large number of species have been observed playing dead in the wild for various reasons.

Main Idea of the Passage _____

Details _____

_____

_____

B   **Listen to part of a lecture about the same topic. Be sure to take notes while you listen.**
   🎧 Q3_08_1

Thesis Statement _____

First Example _____

Details _____

_____

_____

Second Example _____

Details _____

_____

_____

C   Read the question and write your response by using the information in your notes.

> Question The professor talks about the pygmy grasshopper and the cichlid. Explain how their actions are related to tonic immobility.

D   Now, say your response out loud to your partner. Don't look at your writing while you speak.

iBT Practice Test

Question 3 of 4

VOLUME

HELP

NEXT

READING TIME 00:00:45

🎧 Q3_08_3

Inbound Marketing

Some companies have recently begun making use of a technique called inbound marketing. These businesses attempt to gain customers by creating content and experiences that can help them. With inbound marketing, companies may attract customers by providing content that can answer questions about a product the customers may have. It can also provide insights about products which show customers how valuable they are. In addition, customers themselves seek inbound marketing. So companies do not have to search for customers. Instead, customers look for them.

The professor talks about her experience purchasing a vehicle. Explain how it is related to inbound marketing.

PREPARATION TIME
00:00:30

RESPONSE TIME
00:00:60

A Read the following passage. Try to understand what the passage is about. After reading the passage, complete the notes below.

Paranoia

People sometimes feel that they are being threatened by others in some manner. For instance, they may believe that other individuals are observing them closely or are working against them in some manner despite the fact that there is no actual proof of their beliefs. This is paranoia. In some extreme cases, people believe that others are actively trying to cause them harm, are lying to them consistently, or are being unfair to them in some manner. Paranoia can be caused by a number of different factors, including a lack of sleep and too much stress.

Main Idea of the Passage _____

Details _____

_____

_____

B Listen to part of a lecture about the same topic. Be sure to take notes while you listen.
🎧 Q3_09_1

Thesis Statement _____

What Happened _____

Details _____

_____

_____

What Happened Later _____

Details _____

_____

C | Read the question and write your response by using the information in your notes.

Question The professor talks about his friend. Explain how his friend's experience is related to paranoia.

_____

_____

_____

_____

_____

_____

_____

_____

_____

D | Now, say your response out loud to your partner. Don't look at your writing while you speak.

🎧 Q3_09_3

Trauma

Individuals may sometimes undergo distressing experiences such as motor vehicle accidents, physical violence, the loss of a close family member or loved one, and military combat. These incidents tend to happen suddenly and without warning and are typically out of a person's control. These experiences—and others—may cause trauma. Among the symptoms of trauma are extreme fear and anxiety, anger, and shock. Some people respond aggressively toward others in response to trauma. In many cases, these feelings lessen over time; however, some people experience long-term trauma and require medical assistance to improve their conditions.

The professor talks about a traffic accident she was in as a teenager. Explain how her experience is related to trauma.

PREPARATION TIME
00:00:30

RESPONSE TIME
00:00:60

A **Read the following passage. Try to understand what the passage is about. After reading the passage, complete the notes below.**

Repetition

Repetition is the process of repeating something again and again or continually doing an action in order to learn it better. While there are some limitations to repetition, it is a proven method for learning, especially at lower levels. First, it enables people to memorize material and put that information into their long-term memory. In addition, when people repeatedly review material, they can pick up new information which they had previously missed while also gaining new insights, thereby allowing them to understand the material better. This method is often recommended for teachers of children and teenagers.

Main Idea of the Passage _____

Details _____

_____

_____

B **Listen to part of a lecture about the same topic. Be sure to take notes while you listen.**

🎧 Q3_10_1

Thesis Statement _____

What Happened _____

Details _____

_____

What Method the Professor Used _____

Details _____

_____

_____

C | **Read the question and write your response by using the information in your notes.**

> Question The professor talks about teaching at an elementary school. Explain how her actions are related to repetition.

D | **Now, say your response out loud to your partner. Don't look at your writing while you speak.**

🎧 Q3_10_3

Introversion

One of the major basic personality types is introversion. Introverts are individuals who are more comfortable dealing with their own thoughts and ideas than what is going on elsewhere. They prefer to spend time either alone or with one or two individuals as opposed to attending events with a large number of people. While extroverts often seek others with whom they can engage, introverts are much more comfortable turning inward, especially when they are looking to relieve stress or to relax.

The professor talks about his sister. Explain how his sister's personality is related to introversion.

PREPARATION TIME
00:00:30

RESPONSE TIME
00:00:60

Part C

Integrated Speaking Task
Listening and Speaking

Question 4

◪ About the Task

The last question presents only a listening passage—a lecture—and not a reading passage. You need to respond based on what you heard. You are given 20 seconds to prepare your response and 60 seconds to speak.

For **Question 4**, you will listen to a lecture about an academic topic. As in Question 3, topics for this question can be drawn from a variety of fields, including life science, social science, physical science, and the humanities. Again like in Question 3, no prior knowledge is necessary to understand the lecture. After hearing the lecture, you are asked to summarize it and to explain how the examples are connected with the overall topic.

When you answer the question, be sure to focus on what the professor discusses. All of the information you discuss should come from the professor's talk. Even if you possess outside knowledge of the topic, you should not use it. Instead, focus solely on the information that the professor provides and then explain how it relates to the question.

🎧 Q4_00_1

Using points and examples from the talk, describe the characteristics of two types of coal.

PREPARATION TIME
00:00:20

RESPONSE TIME
00:00:60

Listen to part of a lecture in a geology class.

M Professor: One of the most important fossil fuels used today is coal. There are coal-fired power plants all over the country providing heat and electricity for millions of people. Now, uh, several different types of coal exist, but I'd like to focus on just two of them right now. They're bituminous coal and anthracite.

Bituminous . . . uh, that's spelled B-I-T-U-M-I-N-O-U-S . . . is by far the most common type of coal here in the United States. It's a type of sedimentary rock that's fairly soft and contains between seventy-seven and eighty-percent carbon. It ignites fairly easily, but due to the impurities that it contains, it creates smoke when it burns. In the U.S., bituminous coal is utilized for two main purposes: The first is to create electricity at power plants while the second is to produce coke for the steel industry.

As for anthracite, it's the hardest type of coal, which is explained by it containing the greatest percentage of carbon. Anthracite is more than eighty-seven percent carbon, which makes it a purer form of carbon than bituminous coal. As a result, it produces more heat when it burns, and it also doesn't produce any smoke, which means that it burns much more cleanly than bituminous coal and other types of coal. Something else interesting about anthracite is that it's a metamorphic rock, which is unlike every other kind of coal. It actually used to be bituminous coal, but, over time, it transformed into anthracite. In the U.S., anthracite is quite rare and has been discovered only in one small part of the country.

Q4_00_2

The professor lectures to the class that coal is a fossil fuel and that there are many types of it, yet he focuses on just two kinds in his lecture. The first type that he discusses is bituminous coal. He points out that it's a sedimentary rock with a high percentage of carbon. However, because it contains some impurities, it creates smoke whenever it burns. The professor also remarks that bituminous coal is used to make electricity and coke for steel in the United States. As for anthracite, it's a harder type of coal because it contains a greater percentage of carbon. Its high carbon content allows it to burn without producing any smoke, which makes it cleaner than the other types of coal, including bituminous. The professor states that anthracite is a metamorphic rock because it used to be bituminous coal but transformed as time passed.

A | **Listen to a lecture on zoology. Be sure to take notes while you listen.** 🎧 Q4_01_1

Main Topic _____

Main Idea _____

First Example _____

Details _____

_____

_____

_____

Second Example _____

Details _____

_____

_____

_____

B | **Read the question and write your response by using the information in your notes.**

Question Using points and examples from the talk, explain how the polar bear's fur helps it survive in cold temperatures.

_____

_____

_____

_____

_____

_____

_____

_____

_____

_____

C | **Now, say your response out loud to your partner. Don't look at your writing while you speak.**

🎧 Q4_01_3

Using points and examples from the talk, explain how birds can avoid getting too hot in the desert.

PREPARATION TIME
00:00:20

RESPONSE TIME
00:00:60

A | **Listen to a lecture on archaeology. Be sure to take notes while you listen.** 🎧 Q4_02_1

Main Topic _____

Main Idea _____

First Example _____

Details _____

_____

_____

_____

Second Example _____

Details _____

_____

_____

_____

B | Read the question and write your response by using the information in your notes.

> Question Using points and examples from the talk, explain two ways that people search for shipwrecks.

C | Now, say your response out loud to your partner. Don't look at your writing while you speak.

iBT Practice Test

🎧 Q4_02_3

Using points and examples from the talk, explain two ways that animals manage to survive droughts.

PREPARATION TIME
00:00:20

RESPONSE TIME
00:00:60

A | **Listen to a lecture on physiology. Be sure to take notes while you listen.** 🎧 Q4_03_1

Main Topic _____

Main Idea _____

First Example _____

Details _____

_____

_____

_____

Second Example _____

Details _____

_____

_____

_____

B | **Read the question and write your response by using the information in your notes.**

Question Using points and examples from the talk, explain how infants communicate with their parents.

_____

_____

_____

_____

_____

_____

_____

_____

_____

_____

C | **Now, say your response out loud to your partner. Don't look at your writing while you speak.**

🎧 Q4_03_3

Using points and examples from the talk, explain how buildings from the past and the present are different.

PREPARATION TIME
00:00:20

RESPONSE TIME
00:00:60

A | **Listen to a lecture on history. Be sure to take notes while you listen.** 🎧 Q4_04_1

Main Topic _____

Main Idea _____

First Example _____

Details _____

_____

_____

_____

Second Example _____

Details _____

_____

_____

_____

B | Read the question and write your response by using the information in your notes.

Question Using points and examples from the talk, explain two ways that railroads affected the United States in the 1800s.

C | Now, say your response out loud to your partner. Don't look at your writing while you speak.

🎧 Q4_04_3

Using points and examples from the talk, explain two ways that conflicts between employees can be resolved.

PREPARATION TIME
00:00:20

RESPONSE TIME
00:00:60

A   **Listen to a lecture on zoology. Be sure to take notes while you listen.** 🎧 Q4_05_1

Main Topic _____

Main Idea _____

First Example _____

Details _____

_____

_____

_____

Second Example _____

Details _____

_____

_____

_____

B | Read the question and write your response by using the information in your notes.

Question Using points and examples from the talk, describe how deer and honeybees cooperate with others of the same species.

_____

_____

_____

_____

_____

_____

_____

_____

_____

_____

C | Now, say your response out loud to your partner. Don't look at your writing while you speak.

🎧 Q4_05_3

Using points and examples from the talk, describe two qualities of a good teacher.

PREPARATION TIME
00:00:20

RESPONSE TIME
00:00:60

A | **Listen to a lecture on marketing. Be sure to take notes while you listen.** 🎧 Q4_06_1

Main Topic _____

Main Idea _____

First Example _____

Details _____

_____

_____

_____

Second Example _____

Details _____

_____

_____

_____

B | Read the question and write your response by using the information in your notes.

> Question Using points and examples from the talk, explain two ways that companies use advertisements to attract customers.

_____

_____

_____

_____

_____

_____

_____

_____

_____

_____

C | Now, say your response out loud to your partner. Don't look at your writing while you speak.

iBT Practice Test

🎧 Q4_06_3

Using points and examples from the talk, explain two disadvantages of animals living in herds.

PREPARATION TIME
00:00:20

RESPONSE TIME
00:00:60

A | **Listen to a lecture on botany. Be sure to take notes while you listen.** 🎧 Q4_07_1

Main Topic _____

Main Idea _____

First Way _____

Details _____

_____

_____

_____

Second Way _____

Details _____

_____

_____

_____

B Read the question and write your response by using the information in your notes.

> Question Using points and examples from the talk, explain two ways that plants are able to survive in tundra.

C Now, say your response out loud to your partner. Don't look at your writing while you speak.

🎧 Q4_07_3

Using points and examples from the talk, explain two problems that are caused by salmon fish farms.

PREPARATION TIME
00:00:20

RESPONSE TIME
00:00:60

A | **Listen to a lecture on zoology. Be sure to take notes while you listen.** 🎧 Q4_08_1

Main Topic _____

Main Idea _____

First Example _____

Details _____

_____

_____

_____

_____

Second Example _____

Details _____

_____

_____

_____

_____

B | **Read the question and write your response by using the information in your notes.**

> Question Using points and examples from the talk, explain how the grass snake and the blobfish are efficient predators.

_____

_____

_____

_____

_____

_____

_____

_____

C | **Now, say your response out loud to your partner. Don't look at your writing while you speak.**

🎧 Q4_08_3

Using points and examples from the talk, explain how dingoes hunt prey.

PREPARATION TIME
00:00:20

RESPONSE TIME
00:00:60

A ‖ **Listen to a lecture on marketing. Be sure to take notes while you listen.** 🎧 Q4_09_1

Main Topic _____

Main Idea _____

First Type _____

Details _____

_____

_____

_____

_____

Second Type _____

Details _____

_____

_____

_____

_____

B | **Read the question and write your response by using the information in your notes.**

> Question Using points and examples from the talk, explain two types of marketing surveys.

_____

_____

_____

_____

_____

_____

_____

_____

_____

_____

C | **Now, say your response out loud to your partner. Don't look at your writing while you speak.**

iBT Practice Test

🎧 Q4_09_3

Using points and examples from the talk, explain two ways in which some people manipulate the stock market.

PREPARATION TIME
00:00:20

RESPONSE TIME
00:00:60

A | **Listen to a lecture on history. Be sure to take notes while you listen.** 🎧 Q4_10_1

Main Topic _____

Main Idea _____

First Method _____

Details _____

_____

_____

_____

_____

Second Method _____

Details _____

_____

_____

_____

_____

B | **Read the question and write your response by using the information in your notes.**

Question Using points and examples from the talk, explain how sailors in ancient times navigated without using the compass.

_____

_____

_____

_____

_____

_____

_____

_____

_____

_____

C | **Now, say your response out loud to your partner. Don't look at your writing while you speak.**

Q4_10_3

Using points and examples from the talk, explain two ways that exercise can provide people with mental benefits.

PREPARATION TIME
00:00:20

RESPONSE TIME
00:00:60

Actual Test

AT00

Speaking Section Directions

Make sure your headset is on.

This section measures your ability to speak about a variety of topics. You will answer four questions by speaking into the microphone. Answer as completely as possible.

In the first question, you will speak about familiar topics. Your response will be scored on your ability to speak clearly and coherently.

In the next two questions, you will first read a short reading passage. This passage will go away, and you will then listen to a talk on the same topic. You will be asked about the information you have read and heard. You will need to combine information from the reading passage and the talk to provide a complete answer. Your response will be scored on your ability to speak clearly and coherently and how accurately you convey information about what you read and heard.

In the last question, you will listen to part of a lecture. You will be asked about what you have heard. Your response will be scored on your ability to speak clearly and coherently and how accurately you convey information about what you heard.

You may take notes while you read and while you listen to the conversations and lectures. You may use your notes to help prepare your response.

Listen carefully to the directions for each question. The directions will not be written on the screen.

For each question, you will be given a short time to prepare your response (15 to 30 seconds, depending on the question). A clock will show how much preparation time is remaining. When the preparation time is up, you will be told to begin your response. A clock will show how much response time is remaining. A message will appear on the screen when the response time has ended.

🎧 AT01

What would you do if you had some extra money? Would you save it or spend it? Please include specific examples and details to support your explanation.

PREPARATION TIME
00:00:15

RESPONSE TIME
00:00:45

🎧 AT02

School Should Open Snack Bar

During my time at Central University, I have had a wonderful experience. However, I believe that it is possible to improve the school, and one way is by opening a snack bar somewhere on campus. Currently, students have nowhere on the school grounds to go if we feel like enjoying a quick snack between classes or taking a study break. Thus the presence of a snack bar would be rather convenient for students here. It would also provide a number of part-time jobs for students, thereby improving the economic situations of some individuals studying at our university.

Victoria Johnson

Junior

The man expresses his opinion about the letter to the editor in the school newspaper. Explain his opinion and the reasons he gives for holding that opinion.

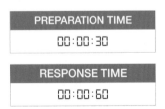

PREPARATION TIME
00:00:30

RESPONSE TIME
00:00:60

 AT03

Buffer Zones

Around the world, humans and animals live in close proximity to one another. However, buffer zones typically separate the two. These regions may enclose an entire area, such as a wildlife refuge, or they may be at the edge of a territory where humans and animals come into contact. Buffer zones are not always entirely uninhabited as there tends to be some mixing of humans and animals. They provide two primary benefits. First, they help humans prevent animals from damaging crops being grown. Second, buffer zones enable animals to thrive in their own ecosystems without any human interference.

The professor talks about Outamba-Kilimi Park. Explain how it is related to buffer zones.

PREPARATION TIME
00:00:30

RESPONSE TIME
00:00:60

AT04

Using points and examples from the talk, explain two ways that insect larvae get food after they hatch.

PREPARATION TIME
00:00:20

RESPONSE TIME
00:00:60

Memo

Authors

Michael A. Putlack

- MA in History, Tufts University, Medford, MA, USA
- Expert test developer of TOEFL, TOEIC, and TEPS
- Main author of the Darakwon *How to Master Skills for the TOEFL® iBT* series and *TOEFL® MAP* series

Stephen Poirier

- Candidate for PhD in History, University of Western Ontario, Canada
- Certificate of Professional Technical Writing, Carleton University, Canada
- Co-author of the Darakwon *How to Master Skills for the TOEFL® iBT* series and *TOEFL® MAP* series

Tony Covello

- BA in Political Science, Beloit College, Beloit, WI, USA
- MA in TEFL, International Graduate School of English, Seoul, Korea
- Term instructor at George Mason University Korea, Songdo, Incheon, Korea

Decoding the **TOEFL**® iBT
SPEAKING Advanced NEW TOEFL® EDITION

Publisher Chung Kyudo
Editor Kim Minju
Authors Michael A. Putlack, Stephen Poirier, Tony Covello
Proofreader Michael A. Putlack
Designers Koo Soojung, Park Sunyoung

First published in October 2021
By Darakwon, Inc.
Darakwon Bldg., 211, Munbal-ro, Paju-si, Gyeonggi-do 10881
Republic of Korea
Tel: 82-2-736-2031 (Ext. 250)
Fax: 82-2-732-2037

Price ₩18,000
ISBN 978-89-277-0886-5 14740
       978-89-277-0875-9 14740 (set)

www.darakwon.co.kr

Components Student Book / Answer Book
7 6 5 4 3 2 1   21 22 23 24 25